His Princess

Love Letters from Your King

by Sheri Rose Shepherd

Multnomah Gifts

Multnomah Books

HIS PRINCESS

© 2004 by Sheri Rose Shepherd
published by Multnomah Books

International Standard Book Number: 978-1-59052-331-5

Design by Koechel Peterson & Assoc., Inc, Minneapolis, Minnesota

Unless otherwise indicated, Scripture quotations are taken from: *Holy Bible,*
New Living Translation ©1996. *The Holy Bible,* New International Version (NIV)
©1973, 1984 by International Bible Society, used by permission of Zondervan
Publishing House. Used by permission of Tyndale House Publishers, Inc. All
rights reserved. *Contemporary English Version* (CEV) © 1995 by American Bible
Society. *New American Standard Bible*® (NASB) ©1960, 1977 by the Lockman
Foundation.

Published in the United States by WaterBrook Multnomah, an imprint of the
Crown Publishing Group, a division of Penguin Random House LLC, New York.

MULTNOMAH and its mountain colophon are registered trademarks
of Penguin Random House LLC.

Printed in China

For Information:
MULTNOMAH PUBLISHERS.
12265 ORACLE BOULEVARD, SUITE 200 • COLORADO SPRINGS, CO 80921

Shepherd, Sheri Rose, 1961–
His princess / by Sheri Rose Shepherd.
p. cm.
ISBN 1-59052-331-8 (Hardcover)
1. Christian women—Prayer-books and devotions—English. I. Title.
BV4844.S534 2004
242'.643—dc22
2003017005

15—21

TABLE OF CONTENTS

"You did not choose Me but I chose you."

JOHN 15:16, NIV

From My Heart to Yours...

RECENTLY I WAS FLYING HOME from speaking at a weekend women's retreat. I leaned back in my seat, exhausted, and began to reflect on the last few days spent with such wonderful women. We laughed, we cried, we ate too much and slept too little. I felt privileged that so many of the ladies felt safe enough to share with me the painful parts of their lives that few had seen.

As I sat there staring out at the clouds below and the heavens above, I wanted desperately to see a miracle in the lives of my new friends. I couldn't help but wonder if anything I said would give Evelyn the encouragement she needed to start over again, help heal Joyce's heart from her past, give Kim the ability to forgive those who hurt her, or provide Jan the strength to get through her trials. Life can be so hard to handle. Could one weekend of truth, transparency, and teaching give them what they needed to complete God's call on their lives?

I began to reflect on my own life and the years I wasted not knowing God's plan, His purpose, and the power that was mine for the asking. I regret the poor choices I made that led me down a road of self-destruction to a life filled with drugs, depression, and eating disorders. In the midst of my misery, I was convinced that all I needed was to lose weight and be pretty and popular. Even after I overcame my addictions and lost weight, I found myself driven by money and success and desperately needing the approval of others. Even achieving a successful career and winning beauty crowns could not complete me.

In the midst of my emptiness and pain, a missionary couple shared with me about the great, eternal crown offered to me by God. I knew I had finally found the answer when I accepted His gift of eternal life, yet it still took me years to truly discover freedom from my past and the call He had on my life. Today, I am a new creation and I have left the past where it belongs…at the cross.

The airplane brought me safely home that weekend, but my heart ached for the countless women who would go home that night feeling anything but safe—or at *home*. With these thoughts tugging at my heart and after reviewing my own life, I realized we can live beyond our pain and our past, our fears and failures, and become…*His princesses*.

I know how hard it is for us to look at our lives

and think of ourselves as *royalty*. But the truth is, God is our King and we are *chosen by Him* (1 Peter 2:9). Unfortunately, many of us have traded the truth of who God says we are for a tarnished version of ourselves, fashioned by the approval of others and adorned with our own insecurities.

I searched the Scriptures over the next few months and wrote what I thought God might say personally to us if we would really hear Him with our heart, take Him at His Word, and have enough faith to believe what He says.

I pray as your soul soaks in these "love letters" that you will never again doubt *who* you are, *why* you are here, and *how* much you are loved.

Love,
Sheri Rose

My Princess...
MY CHOSEN ONE

I chose you before the foundation of the earth to be My princess. You are royalty even when you don't feel like a princess. I will wait for you until you are ready to start living the amazing plans I have for you. I know you don't know where to begin or how to become what I've called you to be, so let Me teach you day by day. Start by recognizing who I am: King of kings and Lord of lords. The Lover of your soul. When the two of us meet alone together every day, I will show you how to let go of the things in your life that are holding you back from the blessings I want to give you.

Remember, My child, just as I have chosen you, I have given you a choice to represent Me to the world. If you are willing, I am here to give you all you need to complete your calling.

Love,

Your King and Lord who chose you

YOU DIDN'T CHOOSE ME, I CHOSE YOU.
I APPOINTED YOU TO GO AND PRODUCE FRUIT
THAT WILL LAST, SO THAT THE FATHER WILL GIVE
YOU WHATEVER YOU ASK FOR, USING MY NAME.

JOHN 15:16

My Princess...
YOU ARE MY PRECIOUS DAUGHTER

*Y*ou are a daughter of the King, and not just any king. You are *My* daughter, and I am the God of all heaven and earth. *I'm delighted with you!* You are the apple of My eye. You're Daddy's girl. Your earthly father may love and adore you, but his love is not perfect, no matter how great—or small—it is. Only *My* love is perfect…because *I am Love.* I formed your body. I fashioned your mind and soul. I know your personality, and I understand your needs and desires. I see your heartaches and disappointments, and I love you passionately and patiently. My child, I bought you with a price so that we could have an intimate relationship together for all eternity. Soon we will see each other face-to-face—Father and daughter—and you will experience the wonderful place I have prepared for you in paradise. Until then, fix your eyes on heaven, and walk closely with Me. You will know that—although I am God—My arms are not too big to hold you, My beloved daughter.

Love,

Your King and your Daddy in heaven

"And I will be your Father,

and you will be my sons and daughters,

says the Lord Almighty."

2 CORINTHIANS 6:18

My Princess...
YOU DON'T HAVE TO FIT IN

I know you want to be accepted by others, but you were not made to fit in. You, My princess, were created to stand out. Not to draw attention to yourself, but to live the kind of life that leads others to Me. Remember, it's your choices that will pave your path to life. I will not force you to do anything. I have given you a free will to walk with Me or to walk away from Me. I want you to know that you can put on your crown at any time and let people know that you belong to Me. You have a royal call on your life. I want you to remember you wear the crown of everlasting life, and through you I will do abundantly more than you would ever dare to dream.

Love,

Your King and Crown Giver

Am I now trying to win
the approval of men,
or of God?
Or am I trying to please men?
If I were still trying to please men,
I would not be a servant of Christ.

GALATIANS 1:10, NIV

The LORD *said:*
It isn't too late.
You can still return to me
with all your heart.

JOEL 2:12, CEV

My Princess...
IT'S NEVER TOO LATE

*I*t is never too late to turn to Me, My love. I didn't start a countdown when I gave you the choice between life and death. There is no time limit on My love for you. I am patient, yet I don't want you to miss out on any precious time with Me. There is no place you have to go to find Me. Just cry out to Me, and I will come to you. Wherever you've gone My grace has followed you. Whatever you've done My blood has covered you. Come to Me today, and I will do more than repair the damage done…I will restore what was lost. Someday you will look back on this moment as the turning point that transformed you into the princess I called you to be. Now come to Me, and let's fall in love all over again.

Love,

Your King who knows no limits

My Princess...
BE MY LIGHT TO
THE WORLD TODAY

I stepped into your darkness so you would shine for Me. Did you know that I have empowered you to light up the lives of everyone around you? You are My light to the world. So walk with Me, and let Me illumine your life today with My love and My power. Look to Me, and I will make you the bright spot in someone's darkness today. Don't hide your light beneath your uncertainties and insecurities. Spend more time with Me and I will make you glow with a godliness that's irresistible. If you will let Me, I'll make you shine in such a way that you will be My star that points to heaven and brings hope to the hurting.

Love,

Your King and True Light of the world

You are the light of the world—
like a city on a mountain,
glowing in the night for all to see.
Don't hide your light under a basket!
Instead, put it on a stand and let it shine for all.

MATTHEW 5:14–15

My Princess...
RUN TO WIN

*Y*ou, My princess, are destined to win. I know how tired you often become, just by trying to do and say all the right things. Take that pressure off yourself, because I did not put it there. The world may judge you by what they see and hear, but I look within your heart, My child. I see your desire to please Me, and I see your struggle to please others. If you want to win this endurance race, you must let go of your need for the approval of others and seek My will and My pleasure. Simplify your life, and let go of the burdens that weigh you down. You'll find that My grace will lighten your step, and My favor will even draw others to join you. Yes, at times you will stumble and fall. But don't worry. I'm here to help you get back up again— as often as it takes. Make it your daily passion to run with Me, and I will carry you over the finish line of your faith. Together we will win!

Love,

Your King and your Champion

Remember that in a race everyone runs,

but only one person gets the prize.

You also must run in such a way

that you will win.

1 CORINTHIANS 9:24

"I AM THE LORD YOUR GOD,
WHO TEACHES YOU
WHAT IS BEST FOR YOU,
WHO DIRECTS YOU IN THE
WAY YOU SHOULD GO."

ISAIAH 48:17, NIV

My Princess...
I AM THE WAY

$\mathcal{T}$he longer you live, the more you will discover there is no other way to have a life that makes a difference apart from Me. I am the one who makes a way where there is no way. I am the one who washes away your sin and gives you a new start over and over again. You may find some pleasure in knowing people or collecting things or accomplishing goals, but it won't be everlasting, My love. The trophies of this world will shine for a season, but all will turn to dust one day. I am the power you need and your purpose for living. No one can give you what I gave you at the cross. I promise, My princess, if you seek Me you will find the secret to everlasting life.

Love,

Your King who makes a way for you

My Princess...
SEE WHAT MATTERS MOST

I have so much to show you, My precious. I know you see the troubles of this world, and they sometimes overwhelm you. So come to Me, and I will take you to the mountaintop. I will open your spiritual eyes so that you may see an eternal view of what matters most. Keep your eyes on Me and in My Word, and you will see My hand at work in everything around you. Remember, My princess, the eyes of the world are on you, so show them who I am by keeping your eyes fixed on Me and My eternal plan for people.

Love,

Your King and Giver of sight

So we don't look at
the troubles we have right now;
rather, we look forward
to what we have not yet seen.
For the troubles we see will soon be over,
but the joys to come will last forever.

2 CORINTHIANS 4:18

My Princess...
HEAR MY VOICE

I am always here for you. I'm never too busy to talk to you, My beloved. If you will turn off the things around you that drown out My voice, you will begin to hear Me in your spirit. When you don't know where to go, you will hear Me give you divine direction. When you are in need of a friend, you will hear Me whisper, "I am here." When you need comfort, you will hear Me call to you, "Come to Me." Don't let the voice of your own uncertainties distract you from My still, small voice. Quiet your spirit, and know that I am your Heavenly Father and you are My precious daughter—and I love when you listen to Me.

Love,

Your King and the Voice of heaven

My sheep listen
to my voice;
I know them,
and they follow me.

JOHN 10:27, NIV

My Princess...
PRAY WITH POWER

*M*y anointed one, you have the power to move a mountain that stands in someone's way. If you will take the time to pray, My power will be released into the lives of those you lift up to Me. I am your King who hears your prayers. As My princess prayer warrior, I've given you authority to call on Me, the God of the universe, to intervene on your behalf! Don't exhaust yourself trying to fix people or problems in your own strength. I am the one who can make a way when there appears to be no way. So don't underestimate the power in your prayer just because your eyes cannot see Me. Call on Me by faith, and know that I will come.

Love,

Your King and Father of miracles

You can ask for anything in my name,

and I will do it, because the work

of the Son brings glory to the Father. Yes, ask

anything in my name, and I will do it!

JOHN 14:13–14

My Princess...
TRIUMPH THROUGH TRIALS

I see you when you are in the garden of grief, My princess. I hear your cry for help in the dark hours of the night. I Myself cried out in the garden the night I was betrayed. In My suffering I asked My Father for another way—a less painful way. Yet I trusted His will and purpose for My life and knew the ultimate victory was at the cross. Just as olives must be crushed to make oil, I poured out My life as a love offering for you. Don't ever doubt that I am with you and that I long to take you to a place of comfort, peace, and victory. Even when you cannot see Me from where you are, I am working on your behalf. Give to Me the crushing weight of your circumstances, and come to Me in prayer. When it is time to leave the garden, I will walk with you across the valley and straight to the cross— where your trials will be transformed into triumph.

Love,

Your Savior and your Victor

For when your faith is tested,
your endurance has a chance to grow.
So let it grow, for when our endurance
is fully developed,
you will be strong in character
and ready for anything.

JAMES 1:3-4

PURIFY ME FROM MY SINS,

AND I WILL BE CLEAN; WASH ME,

AND I WILL BE WHITER THAN SNOW.

PSALM 51:7

My Princess...
TREASURE YOUR BODY

*Y*our body is a gift from Me, and you are too valuable to let the wrong person open that gift. You are My treasure, and My Spirit dwells within you. I know there is an inner war raging for your soul and your body—fighting against all you know to be true. Remember, My love, I can fight this battle for you, so don't compromise My best for you for a moment of passion. I know it may seem harmless to give yourself away, but the pain is not worth the pleasure. Listen, My love: Don't imitate those in the world who care nothing for your soul. Give yourself to Me, and I will give you the love you're looking for.

Love,

Your King and your Purity

My Princess...
YOU ARE FORGIVEN FOREVER

*M*y love, I willingly gave My life here on earth and died for you. I went to a cross as your King so that your sins would be forgiven and so you would receive a crown. Not just any crown, but the crown of everlasting life. If you refuse to receive the gift of forgiveness that comes from Me, then you are saying My death isn't enough to cover your sin. Please, My princess, let go of your guilt and forgive yourself and those who have hurt you. In due time I will repay those who hurt you if they don't repent and do what is right. In the meantime you are free…you are forgiven. Once you've confessed your sin to Me, I cast it into the sea of My forgetfulness—never to see or remember it again. So let go and live a free and full life, My precious one.

Love,
Your King, Jesus

O Lord, you are so good,

so ready to forgive,

so full of unfailing love

for all who ask your aid.

PSALM 86:5

*S*ee I am coming soon
and my reward is with me
to repay all
according to their deeds.

REVELATION 22:12

My Princess...
YOU WILL BE
GREATLY REWARDED

I see you when no one else does. I see you meet others needs when no one is looking. I know when you give generously when there is no spotlight. Your name may never be on a plaque for the world to notice, but I see you, My faithful one. I know you need to be appreciated for who you are and all you do. But don't give up. I will bring you a reward that can't be bought in a store or found in the praises of people. I can't wait to celebrate in heaven all you have done to further My kingdom. I'm so pleased with your dedication and good works. Until that great day—when I exalt you and your good works for the whole world to see—let Me give you a taste of those blessings here on earth. Thank you for your faithfulness, My princess. The best is yet to come.

Love,

Your King and your Rewarder

My Princess...
FOLLOW ME

*Y*our feet are beautiful when they follow Me. I am the Way, the Truth, and the Life, My love, and I have given you feet to walk with Me through this life. Just as Moses walked My people out of slavery, your walk with Me will be filled with My divine intervention. If you follow My lead, you will feel Me as we journey together in the same direction. I want you to keep your feet on the narrow road, and I will anoint you to take My life-giving news to others. You will have the courage to tell them that I am the God who gives salvation to all who want to know Me. Keep walking with Me, My princess, because you carry My life-changing truth inside your soul.

Love,

Your King and your Deliverer

How beautiful on the mountains
are the feet of those who bring good news
of peace and salvation, the news
that the God of Israel reigns!

ISAIAH 52:7

My Princess...
YOU ARE MY TRUE BEAUTY

*Y*our real beauty is a work of art—hand carved by Me. I have given you beautiful lips to speak words of life, beautiful eyes to see Me in everything, beautiful hands to help those in need, and a beautiful face to reflect My love to the world. I know you don't see yourself the way I do because you compare yourself to beauty idols that will soon be forgotten. I will work wonders that will radiate true beauty from within. And when My work is completed, your character will show off My craftsmanship, and your beauty marks will be remembered by all that were loved by you.

Love,

Your radiant King

Our daughters will be like pillars

carved to adorn a palace.

PSALM 144:12, NIV

My Princess...
I'M WITH YOU IN
TIMES OF TROUBLE

*Y*ou never need to doubt if I am in the midst of your circumstances. No matter how hot the fire seems, the flames will not scorch you as long as I am present. Just as I was with Shadrach, Meshach, and Abednego in their fiery test of faith, I am here now with you, ready to cool you off and keep you calm as we walk through this trial together. You may not see it now, but you, My princess, will someday be like precious silver that has been refined by fire and purified in My presence. Remember, I did not put you in a fire to burn you out. Trust Me with your troubled heart, and watch Me do wonders for you in the midst of the hottest flames.

Love,

Your King and your Refiner

THE LORD IS MY STRENGTH, MY SHIELD
FROM EVERY DANGER. I TRUST IN HIM
WITH ALL MY HEART. HE HELPS ME,
AND MY HEART IS FILLED WITH JOY.

PSALM 28:7

My Princess...
FREEDOM IS A CHOICE

I long to give you the keys to be free from the things that bind you and see you break through to a blessed life in Me. But your freedom is a choice…*your* choice. You can be totally free in Me or try to set yourself free. I promise, My princess, I am the only One who can give you the life-giving keys you need and want. The keys are hidden in My Word, empowered by your prayer, and completed by the work of My Holy Spirit living in you. Choose the way, My love…choose life.

Love,

Your King and your freedom

So if the Son sets you free,
you will be free indeed .

JOHN 8:36, NIV

My Princess...
TRUST ME WITH
THOSE YOU LOVE

I know your heart, and I know how much you love those close to you. I am your Creator and the Giver of every good gift. I have given you loved ones to share your life with. But you, My child, must remember that those you love ultimately belong to Me—not to you. I didn't give you those special relationships to tear you apart or to control you through fear of the future. Like Abraham did with his only son, Isaac, I need you to open your heart and give back to Me those you love. Trust Me with everything that concerns you regarding them. Place your hand in Mine, and I promise I will walk you—and your loved ones— through all things this life brings.

Love,

Your trustworthy King

Those who trust in the LORD

are secure as Mount Zion;

they will not be defeated

but will endure forever.

PSALM 125:1

My Princess...
I WILL REDEEM
THE TIME FOR YOU

I know that sometimes you look back on your life with anguish and regret—so much time wasted on things that did not matter. But take heart, My love. I am your Redeemer, and today is a new day. So start now by seeking My plans, which are to give you hope and a future. Just as I used hardship in Joseph's life to lead him to a position of leadership, influence, and blessing, I've also called you. I will use your past to carve into your character everything you need for the here and now. I want you to let your past experiences teach you and not torment you. Remember, My princess, I will always turn into good what others meant for harm. I will redeem what was lost and place you on the narrow road that leads to an everlasting life.

Love,

Your King and your Redeemer

"FOR I KNOW THE PLANS I HAVE FOR YOU,"
DECLARES THE LORD, "PLANS TO PROSPER
YOU AND NOT TO HARM YOU,
PLANS TO GIVE YOU HOPE AND A FUTURE."

JEREMIAH 29:11, NIV

My Princess...
CHOOSE YOUR BATTLES

*E*very day can be a fight for something or with someone if you so choose. I want you, My princess warrior, to choose your battles wisely, and fight for the things worth fighting for. There are so many things that stand against you in the battlefield, and there are so many worthy causes. But the enemy of your soul will entice you to fight the wrong battles in order to distract you from your main mission. Remember, My beloved, your fight is not against flesh and blood, but against evil forces in the spiritual realm. When you find yourself in the midst of a war, do not be afraid. Call on Me in prayer and allow Me to deliver you. In My timing, I will give you the victory and bring justice to the afflicted. So don't waste your time fighting the wrong battles. And never forget that the spiritual war is fought—and won—on your knees.

Love,

Your Warrior King

For the Lord your God
is the one who goes with you
to fight for you against
your enemies to give you victory.

DEUTERONOMY 20:4, NIV

*E*ach of you has been blessed
with one of God's many wonderful gifts
to be used in the service of others.
So use your gift well.

1 PETER 4:10, CEV

My Princess...
YOU ARE MY GIFTED ONE

I have given you the gift of eternal life, but My giving does not stop there. Inside of you is a supernatural surprise—a gift that is waiting to be unwrapped…by *you*.

Yes, it's there. It's hidden behind dreams waiting to be pursued. Swallowed up by daily distractions and drowned by disappointment.

Let Me help you clear out the clutter and find your gift. You'll find it in that place in life that brings you the greatest joy, that place where your soul longs to be, that work your hands love to do.

But this gift that I've given to you is not just *for* you. I have blessed you to be a blessing to others. When you find your gift, I will take it and multiply it beyond what you could ever imagine. So ask Me, and I will help you open your gift so that you can give it away to the world—not to impress—but to bless.

Love,

Your King and the Giver
of every good and perfect gift

My Princess...
YOUR LIFE IS A SYMPHONY

*Y*ou are to Me a beautiful song. Your life is a sweet symphony that I Myself am composing note by note. I take your failures, your tears, and your triumphs, and I turn them into a glorious harmony that will be sung in the heavens for all eternity. All your thoughts and deeds are laid before Me like notes on a page. Every choice you make is a significant chord in an eternal arrangement. Don't let the noise of the world destroy your magnificent melody, My beloved. Seek Me in the quiet stillness of the morning, and I will fill your heart with divine music. Stay in rhythm with My Spirit throughout the day, and I will make your life an irresistible medley that will linger like sweet perfume in the hearts of all that journey with you. Walk with Me in absolute surrender, and you will draw others to Me in a rhapsody of praise.

Love,

Your King and your Composer

He has given me a new song to sing,

a hymn of praise to our God.

Many will see what he has done

and be astounded. They will

put their trust in the Lord.

PSALM 40:3, NIV

My Princess...
FILL YOUR HOME
WITH PEACE

I know how hard it is for you to feel content in your home when you're always wanting one more thing to make it the perfect place. I long to give you beautiful things that turn a house into the haven of a home; but My princess, you must first learn to let Me build *in you* a place of peace and contentment. Do your best to rest in Me and wait for Me, and then I will give you what I know will benefit you the most. I want you to make your home a place that builds relationships and reflects who you are in Me. Remember that your loved ones need you more than any material thing. So decorate your home with joy, fill it with timeless memories, and create a safe place to grow up in Me.

Love,

Your King and your Resting Place

PEACE I LEAVE WITH YOU;
MY PEACE I GIVE YOU. I DO NOT GIVE
AS THE WORLD GIVES. DO NOT
LET YOUR HEARTS BE TROUBLED....

JOHN 14:27, NIV

I WILL STRENGTHEN YOU.

I WILL HELP YOU.

I WILL UPHOLD YOU WITH

MY VICTORIOUS RIGHT HAND.

ISAIAH 41:10

My Princess...
YOU HAVE BEAUTIFUL HANDS

*Y*our hands are beautiful because they are blessed by Me. I want you to raise your hands to heaven and praise Me. Ask Me, and I will anoint your hands to heal those who are hurting and help those who are in need. I have given you those beautiful hands to touch others with My love, and when you use your hands to work for My kingdom, I will bless all that you do. It is a privilege, My princess, to have that kind of power in your possession. I can do amazing things through you when you faithfully hold on to My promises. Be assured that while you are using your hands to help others, I, your King, will move My mighty hand in all areas of your life. So keep reaching out to the world, My love, and help them to know that I am real. Hold on to My hand, and know that I will never let you go.

Love,

Your King and the One who holds your hand

My Princess...
SPEAK LIFE WITH MY WORDS

*M*y child, I love your mouth because it is Mine—
ready to be filled with My words. Did you know that
I've anointed your beautiful lips with the power to
speak life to a lifeless world? While others are using
their lips to spread worthless words, you, My princess,
have the privilege of changing people's perspectives
and empowering them to make life changing choices
that point them to Me. Your words will be more valuable than priceless jewels. I want you to come to Me
in prayer every day, I will line your lips with love,
wisdom, and encouragement and make your mouth
My masterpiece for all who see you speak.

Love,

Your King and Counselor

*L*et the words of Christ, in all their richness,
live in your hearts and make you wise.
Use his words to teach and counsel each other.
Sing psalms and hymns and spiritual songs to God
with thankful hearts. And whatever you do or say,
let it be as a representative of the Lord Jesus.

COLOSSIANS 3:16-17

My Princess...
WALK IN MY
CONFIDENCE

I know the world whispers in your ear that what you possess defines who you are, and what you look like determines your worth. This is a lie, My love. The generations to come will never remember you for the things you accumulate or the efforts you placed in your appearance. In fact, the harder you strive to collect more things and to perfect your image, the more insecure you will be about who you are and why you are here. I am in you and you are in Me. I will give you all that you need. Now go and walk through your world in the confidence that I've uniquely equipped you with all you need to impact the lives of those around you forever!

Love,

Your King and your Confidence

FOR THE LORD WILL BE YOUR CONFIDENCE,
AND WILL KEEP YOUR FOOT
FROM BEING CAUGHT.

PROVERBS 3:26, NASB

My Princess...
I WILL PROTECT YOU

I am your shield of protection. Many times you wonder where I am in the midst of the battle that rages around you. You feel abandoned on the battlefield. Don't be afraid and don't lose faith. I am here, and I am *always* victorious. I will protect you, but you must trust Me. Sometimes I will lead you to shelter for safety and restoration. Other times I will ask you to join Me on the front line in the heat of the battle. The truth is, I can kill any giant that threatens your life, but, just like David the shepherd boy, it's up to you to march forward, pick up the stones, and face your giant. I love to prove My strength when the odds are the greatest and hope is the smallest. I am truly your shelter and your deliverer—I will protect you no matter where you are.

Love,

Your King and your Protector

You are my hiding place;

you will protect me from trouble

and surround me with songs of deliverance.

PSALM 32:7, NIV

My Princess...
DON'T EVER COMPROMISE

*I*n your weakness, I will keep you strong, My child. I am well aware of the many things in this life that war against your spirit and your soul. I know it feels like distractions and difficulties are sent daily to test your character and convictions. Remember, My love, this life is not a dress rehearsal. It's the real thing, and I'm training you through these tests to trust Me. I am preparing you today for your future life in heaven. So seek Me in prayer for My strength, and don't give in to temptation or compromise. They are like quicksand lying on your path to righteousness. Hold on to Me and My power within you, and I promise that you will make it through. When the wicked winds try to blow out the flame of your faith or try to cause you to compromise, stand on My truth...I am your solid Rock, and you can conquer anything in My strength.

Love,

Your King and your Rock

Temptations that come
into your life are no different
from what others experience.
And God is faithful.
He will keep the temptation
from becoming so strong
that you can't stand up against it.
When you are tempted,
he will show you a way out
so that you will not give in to it.

1 CORINTHIANS 10:13

My Princess...
GROW WHERE YOU ARE PLANTED

I know you sometimes wonder if your life has any real worth. But I assure you that I can use you to impact those around you. Just as I used Paul in prison I will use you wherever you are or whatever circumstance you are in. Let Me water you with My holy Word, and you will begin to bloom wherever you are planted. Come to Me in prayer and let Me empower you with My spirit. Even if you can't see the harvest of your hard work now, I promise that others will one day look back at the time you were in their lives and remember your acts of kindness, words of wisdom, and love for them. So for now, My valuable princess, let Me help you blossom in a world that is searching for the meaning of life.

Love,
Your King and Gardener of Life

And we know that God
causes everything to work together
for the good of those who love God
and are called according to
his purpose for them.

ROMANS 8:28

My Princess...
WAIT ON ME

*W*ait on Me, My princess. My timing is always perfect. I know you're anxious about many things, and I see your passion for all the plans I have put in your heart. I know that you long to fly, and I see your enthusiasm. However, just as a vinedresser nurtures the vine and waits patiently for the right moment to harvest the grapes, so too am I working tirelessly to prepare you to bear much fruit. Don't run ahead of Me or try to fly before My plans are complete. Your strength will fail you, and your dreams will wither away. Trust Me that My dreams for you are far greater than you can dream on your own. You will run farther and soar higher if you will patiently wait for the season of My blessing. Draw close to Me now, and I promise that this season of waiting will bring you the sweetest of rewards.

Love,
Your King and Lord of perfect timings

BUT THOSE WHO WAIT ON THE LORD
WILL FIND NEW STRENGTH. THEY WILL FLY HIGH
ON WINGS LIKE EAGLES. THEY WILL RUN AND
NOT GROW WEARY. THEY WILL WALK AND NOT FAINT.

ISAIAH 40:31, NIV

*Do not be afraid, for I have ransomed you.
I have called you by name; you are mine.
When you go through deep waters
and great trouble, I will be with you.
When you go through rivers of difficulty,
you will not drown!"*

ISAIAH 43:1–2

My Princess...
I WILL HEAL YOUR HEART

*D*on't get discouraged, My beloved; pain is a part of life. But I promise you that I will turn every tear you've cried into joy, and I will use your deep pain for a divine purpose. Don't try to hide your hurts from Me. I know everything about you. You are Mine, My beloved! I'm the only one who can handle your heart and restore you to health and wholeness again. I, too, have felt great pain, rejection, and anger. But we can go through every trial together. Hand in hand I will lead you back to My place of peace and joy after the storm. The sun will shine on you again, and your heart will be healed. I promise you, My Princess, that when you go through deep waters of great trouble, I will be with you. When you go through rivers of difficulty you will not drown. When you walk through the fire of oppression you will not be burned.

Love,

Your King and your Healer

"BE STRONG AND COURAGEOUS!
DO NOT BE AFRAID OF THEM!
THE LORD YOUR GOD WILL GO
AHEAD OF YOU. HE WILL NEITHER
FAIL YOU NOR FORSAKE YOU."

DEUTERONOMY 31:6

My Princess...
TAKE COURAGE IN ME

*Y*ou need never be afraid to stand up and do what is right, My child. I will always go ahead of you and prepare the way. I rescued Daniel from the mouth of the lions and delivered David from the hands of his enemies. Can you trust that I am strong enough to handle any situation? I truly want what is best for you. Take courage and walk in My strength, not your own. Face every situation head-on—armed with the sword of the Spirit, the belt of truth, the armor of righteousness, and the shield of faith. You never need to turn your back and run—I will empower you and protect you. Just stand firm and pray, and watch your courage become contagious.

Love,

Your King and your Captain of courage

My Princess...
I CAME TO SERVE YOU

*E*ven when you don't feel valued, let Me remind
you, My Princess, that I—your King—came to serve
you. I not only created you; I also sustain your life,
comfort your spirit, and provide what you need. You
are so valuable that I even paid the ultimate price at
the cross to ransom you, My child. I am able to take
any failure or mistake you've made and miraculously
use it for My glory. I am patient, kind, and merciful—
I am Love. So now that you know your sins are forgiven, I am asking you to turn from who you were
and become who I called you to be. Let Me help you.
I am your Lord who loves you no matter what.

Love,

Your King who came for you

"For even I, the Son of Man,
came here not to be served
but to serve others,
and to give my life
as a ransom for many."

MATTHEW 20:28

My Princess...

WALK THE ROAD
TO LIFE

There will always be two roads before you, My love. The popular road is easy, its bumps worn smooth by the wandering crowds. This road appears safe simply because so many have already ventured around its curves and shuffled down into its valleys. What the crowds don't understand is that this road is filled with regret and guilt, and it ultimately leads to death. This is the road that leads away from Me, your King. If you find yourself on the wrong path, don't lose heart—just cry out to Me and I will find you. I won't join you on this destructive detour, but I will lead you back to the road that leads to life again—the road your feet were created to walk on. Throughout My Word you will find signposts that will give you wisdom and direction. So keep reading and walking, My princess, and you will begin to discover the real joy of the journey of life.

Love,

Your King and the Way, the Truth, and the Life

BE CAREFUL TO OBEY ALL THE COMMANDS I GIVE
YOU; SHOW LOVE TO THE LORD YOUR GOD BY
WALKING IN HIS WAYS AND CLINGING TO HIM.

DEUTERONOMY 11:22, NIV

My Princess...
DRESS LIKE ROYALTY

I've called you to be royalty, My princess. You don't have to conform to the wardrobes of this world to feel good about yourself. Remember, what you wear initially defines what people think about you. I want your wardrobe to honor *Me*. You don't need to dress to get attention—I can make you more beautiful than any fashion designer because I specialize in *internal* and *eternal* makeovers. Your favor and beauty will radiate because you are a reflection of Me. Keep in mind that those who design clothes to expose your body do not love your soul like I do. My love, let your wardrobe reveal *My* spirit—not *your* flesh. So robe yourself today like the royalty you are.

Love,

Your King and your eternal beauty

*Charm can be deceiving
and beauty fades away,
but a woman who honors the* Lord
deserves to be praised.

PROVERBS 31:30, CEV

My Princess...
DO NOT FEAR

*A*re you bound up in darkness and fear? Come to Me and tell Me what you're afraid of. Is it the future? your health? your circumstances? your finances? your security? Don't you know that I am Creator and King of all? I own all the resources in the universe. Nothing is beyond My knowledge or My power. Remember that I am your God and Salvation. I will never give you more than you can handle. Ask Me about anything with faith and obey what I tell you to do, and you will feel your fear vanish. I am the Lord your God, and I delight in caring for you, My child. So do not fear, My princess. I am always near.

Love,

Your King and your Fearless Leader

The LORD is my light and my salvation—

so why should I be afraid?

The LORD protects me from danger—

so why should I tremble?

PSALM 27:1

My Princess...
KNOW THE TRUTH

*L*et Me take you back to the beginning of our relationship. Do you remember when you asked Me to be
your Lord and King? I do, because I wrote your name
in My Book of Life at that very moment, and you
entered into a love relationship with Me. All the
angels rejoiced in heaven!

Our relationship can never be destroyed by anything or anyone. Once you were lost but now you are
found, and My Spirit lives in you—you are Mine! I
don't want you to let life's craziness and confusion
distract you from knowing Me personally. So
remember the truth—stand on it, read it, pray it, obey
it, and walk in the wonderful truth that you are My
princess, My chosen one!

Love,

Your King and your Truth

Jesus said to the people who believed in Him,

"You are truly my disciples

if you keep obeying my teachings.

And you will know the truth,

and the truth will set you free."

JOHN 8:31–32

My Princess...
I AM YOUR PEACE

I long to give you rest for your soul and peace in your heart. I know sometimes it looks like life has no peace to offer—just one big problem after another. It's true that the world is filled with hatred, envy, and every sort of evil, so please don't be looking for peace in *people* or attempting to position yourself where there are no problems. The kind of peace the world tries to offer is built on false hope and man-made idols that will eventually crumble. The peace I give you will transcend any trial or tribulation that comes against you because it is *supernatural*. So position yourself completely in My care, and let go of all those things you cannot control. Then you will find true peace. In the middle of chaos and confusion, I will always be your safe place—a place of peace. I'm asking you, My princess, to share with others the peace I give freely to you.

Love,
Your King and your Perfect Peace

*P*eace I leave with you;
my peace I give you.
I do not give to you as the world gives.
Do not let your hearts be troubled
and do not be afraid.

JOHN 14:27, NIV

My Princess...
COME TO ME

I saw you before you were born. Even then you were on My mind, My daughter. I knew you were coming, and I did everything possible to express My love to you and extend My invitation to you. Now that you are Mine, I want you to continue to come to Me. Come to Me when you feel strong and when you feel weary. Come to Me when you are rejoicing and when your spirit is crushed. I ask you to come not only to give you rest, but also because there is so much more I want to teach you. There is more of Me I want to reveal to you. You see, I did not create you for this fallen world. I created you for Paradise, but the curse of sin tore us apart. I've conquered sin and death for you through the death of My son, so come to Me…and live.

Love,
Your King who is waiting

"Come to me, all of you who are weary and
carry heavy burdens, and I will give you rest.
Take my yoke upon you. Let me teach you,
because I am humble and gentle,
and you will find rest for your souls."

MATTHEW 11:28–29

My Princess...
YOU HAVE GREAT TREASURES IN HEAVEN

I am so looking forward to giving you amazing treasures in heaven. I am coming soon, My love, and when I do, I will have your reward with Me. I love to bless your life here on earth, but your eyes haven't seen nor has your heart yet experienced the gifts of eternal joy and blessing that I have waiting for you above. For now, My sweet princess, make every moment count, because what you do today echoes throughout eternity. Like ripples in a pond, your hard work and faithfulness to Me spread far beyond this life and into forever. Remember that no amount of money can buy you the great gifts you will open when we are finally together on the other side of eternity.

Love,

Your King and Eternal Treasure

"See, I am coming soon,
and my reward is with me,
to repay all according to their deeds.
I am the Alpha and the Omega, the First
and the Last, the Beginning and the End."

REVELATION 22:12–13

Let us be glad and rejoice and honor him.
For the time has come for the wedding feast of the
Lamb, and his bride has prepared herself.

REVELATION 19:7

My Princess...
YOU ARE MY BEAUTIFUL BRIDE

*Y*ou are My beautiful bride! There is a day coming when we will rejoice together in heaven. No wedding on earth can compare to the celebration we will share on that amazing day! Every bride prepares for her earthly wedding by doing all she can to be her best. The bride's attendants work diligently to make everything perfect before she meets her bridegroom. My princess, I am your heavenly Bridegroom, and I have already made all the preparations for you. Don't worry that your life is not perfect. On that glorious wedding day, I will present you spotless and blameless for all of heaven to see. All I ask of you today is that your heart be fully and completely Mine. Let My faithfulness, mercy, and love be the sweet music that fills the wedding sanctuary. You, My bride, will be clothed in a beautiful gown of My glory on that great day, and all the depths and heights of heaven's joy will be yours.

Love,
Your King and your Bridegroom

My Princess...
YOU ARE FREE TO LOVE

I have set you free to love others, so don't let people who have caused you pain paralyze you from experiencing the joys of love. I know there is always a risk when you give a piece of your heart away, but I've created you to enjoy the gift of special friendships. Choose wisely the ones that you invest your time and energy in, and also give those you love the freedom to fail. Remember that no one will love you as perfectly as I do. If you let Me take the disappointments that come with relationships, you will be free to give and receive love unconditionally. Remember, My princess, most people need love the *most* when they deserve it the *least*.

Love,

Your King who is Love

Most important of all,
continue to show deep love for each other,
for love covers a multitude of sins.

1 PETER 4:8

My Princess...
GIVE ME YOUR PLANS

I know you have an idea in your head on how everything should unfold in your life. Even today you have an agenda. Because I love you, I need you to give Me back all your plans for today and for all your tomorrows. If you let Me have your day, I can then intervene with something special. My intervention will give you more joy in your journey than your good intentions. I know all that your heart longs for, and I want to do more for you than you could ever do for yourself. So give Me a chance to change your agenda from ordinary to extraordinary, because that's the kind of life I've destined you to live, My beloved.

Love,

Your King and your Planner

Commit to the Lord whatever you do,
and your plans will succeed.

PROVERBS 16:3, NIV

My Princess...
I CAN DO ANYTHING

I know how hard it is for you to believe that My power is for you personally. The only thing stopping you from seeing My mighty hand at work in your life is you, My love. Remember, I placed within you the same power that I used to raise My Son, Jesus, from the dead. Don't let past disappointments or fears keep you from asking what you need and believing that My timing is perfect. Keep seeking Me with all your heart and continue to obey all that I say while you wait on Me. Know that I will always keep My word and fulfill My promises. Even when the world lets you down, I will lift you up again. I will be true to you until the end of time and beyond.

Love,

Your True King

> THE LORD ANSWERED,
> "I CAN DO ANYTHING!
> WATCH AND YOU'LL SEE
> MY WORDS COME TRUE."
>
> NUMBERS 11:23, CEV

My Princess...
YOU ARE CONNECTED TO ME

I am the vine—your spiritual lifeline—and you are My beautiful branch that produces fruit for all to taste. I am in you and with you. We are eternally connected. You will never feel alone or abandoned as long as you stay connected to Me. Wherever you are I am there, ready to give you whatever you need for that moment in time. I delight in flowing through you, My precious one. I will never disconnect our relationship even if you try to run from Me. My loving arms are always open to welcome you home. Always remember that nothing you do or say will ever change My love for you. So stay close to the Vine, My love.

Love,

Your King and your Vinedresser

"Yes, I am the vine;
you are the branches.
Those who remain in me,
and I in them,
will produce much fruit.
For apart from me you can do nothing."

JOHN 15:5

"AND BE SURE OF THIS:

I AM WITH YOU ALWAYS,

EVEN TO THE END OF THE AGE."

MATTHEW 28:20

My Princess...
YOU'RE NEVER ALONE

*Y*ou never need to hold on to anyone out of fear of being alone, My precious princess. I am with you wherever you are. I am the friend who walks in when the world walks out. I created you to have strong relationships, My love, and I see your desire to be close to someone. If you will seek Me first and come to Me with your wants and needs, I will choose your friends for you. I also will bless those friendships abundantly. Don't settle for less than My best just to fill your schedule with people to see and places to go. I want to reach you with the reality of My presence in you first, and then you will be ready for *real* relationships that are orchestrated by Me.

Love,

Your King and your Best Friend

My Princess...
LET ME OPEN YOUR SPIRITUAL EYES

Come to Me right now, and let Me open your spiritual eyes as I did for Elisha's servant when a deadly army surrounded him. With his spiritual eyes he could see an entire host of My heavenly warriors and chariots of fire there to protect him. You are also My chosen one, and I promise to protect you if you will walk by faith in the midst of your daily battles. Don't forget that there is an unseen enemy of your soul who will try to cause you to stumble, so let Me be your eyes when you cannot see. And remember, "Greater is he that is in you, than he that is in the world" (1 John 4:4). I am He. I am the one who fights for you. Even when you feel like you are in the middle of a war, the battle is not yours—it is Mine. So let Me open your eyes of faith, and you will see that the victory is won.

Love,

Your King who gives you sight

For we are not fighting
against people made of flesh and blood,
but against the evil rulers
and authorities of the unseen world . . .
and against wicked spirits
in the heavenly realms.

EPHESIANS 6:12

And the peace of God,
which transcends all understanding,
will guard your hearts and
your minds in Christ Jesus.

PHILIPPIANS 4:7, NIV

My Princess...
GUARD YOUR MIND

I want your mind fixed on Me, My beloved. But I want even more from you. I desire great things for you, so I want you to guard your mind by making an "aware list"—all the things you watch, listen to, and read. Let Me show you the things that can carry you away from your calling and destroy your dedication to Me. Even your thoughts can be held captive by the ways of the world. I want to protect you, but I will never force you to listen to My Spirit or make your mind dwell on what is true, pure, and right. The choice is yours, My love. You *can* have an abundant life, a blessed life—a life of influence for others to follow; or you can join the way of the world. I, your God, am asking you today to let your mind dwell on Me, and you will discover the kind of life you long to enjoy not only now, but forever.

Love,

Your King and your Peace of Mind

"And who knows but that

you have come to royal position

for such a time as this?"

ESTHER 4:14, NIV

My Princess...
I WILL UPHOLD YOU

I have raised you up to a place of great purpose, but there will be many who will not understand your position. Even you may not realize why I have strategically placed you here *for such a time as this.* You will be tempted to seek the approval of others and waste precious time defending the plans that I've placed in your heart. Remember, I am the Lord your God. You did not choose Me…I chose you. I will lift you high above any circumstances that come against My divine purpose for your life. The only one who can stop My miraculous work in and through your life is *you.* So instead of making one more plan, give your plans completely to Me, and let Me finish the work I started in you.

Love,

Your King and your Divine Purpose

My Princess...
PRAY WITH POWER

*M*y powerful princess, do not waste your walk through life today. Open your spiritual eyes. Prayer is needed everywhere. Anywhere you walk today I can and will order your steps, if you will let Me. Pray while you're driving, while you're cooking, and while you're doing laundry and running errands. Of all the weapons in the world, prayer is your most powerful resource. Don't let the day begin or end without letting your prayers to Me pave the way in all you do. Wherever you go, remember that part of your royal privilege is raising your voice to heaven. So hold on to the promises that are yours and pray!

Love,

Your King and Intercessor

PRAY AT ALL TIMES AND ON EVERY OCCASION
IN THE POWER OF THE HOLY SPIRIT. STAY ALERT
AND BE PERSISTENT IN YOUR PRAYERS
FOR ALL CHRISTIANS EVERYWHERE.

EPHESIANS 6:18

My Princess...
LET ME BUILD A TRUE FRIENDSHIP

I want you to look for a true friend—not just any friend. Find someone who brings out the best in you—a girlfriend who is a gift from Me. My love, it takes time to build a strong foundation with a true friend, so choose your tools wisely. The first tool you'll need is *transparency*…the ability to see within each other's heart—your strengths and weaknesses. The next tool is *truth.* I am the way, the truth, and the life for you. You will discover the rewards of real friendships when you speak truth and bring refreshing words of encouragement to each other. Finally, your friendship will need to be sealed in *love,* girded with *trust,* and encircled with *prayer.* Remember, My princess, you must become the kind of friend you desire to have.

Love,
Your King and True Friend

Some friends don't help,

but a true friend

is closer than your own family.

PROVERBS 18:24, CEV

My Princess...
I WILL SET YOU FREE

I, your King, stand outside the door of your heart and knock. I see you locked up in your private place of pain, but I won't force My way in. I will continue to wait patiently outside until you're ready to let Me come in. I long to hold you in My arms, wipe away your tears, and tenderly encourage you with My love and truth. I will continue to knock even when you turn a deaf ear. I won't stop calling to you from outside the door of your prison of pain. You do not have to answer, but I won't give up because I love you. I know your heart's cry is for the wholeness and healing that only I can bring. It's not too late, My princess. Today you can unlock the door in the darkened room of your heart and let Me come in. Like warm light and a gentle breeze, I will refresh and nourish your soul.

Love,

Your King and your Key to Freedom

Listen! I am standing
and knocking at your door.
If you hear my voice and open the door,
I will come in and we will eat together.

REVELATION 3:20, CEV

My Princess...
YOU ARE SAVED BY GRACE

*D*on't be so hard on yourself, My love. I see your heart filled with frustration. I know you're in a constant battle between your flesh and your spirit. Don't ever give up trying to live out your faith because of your weaknesses. Don't you know that nothing you do in your own strength will last? I give you grace when you've gone the wrong way, and I give you strength right when you need it. I am here waiting to make all your wrongs right and to heal all your hurts. The battles in your mind belong to Me, so don't waste any more time tearing yourself down. I love you no matter what you've done or said. Now give Me a chance to show you who you are when you are surrendered to Me. Let Me give you My gift of grace. Remember that you have been covered with My forgiveness since Calvary; now walk in freedom from the past and open My gift of a new start.

Love,
Your King and your Grace

For all have sinned
and fall short of the glory of God,
and are justified freely by his grace through
the redemption that came by Christ Jesus.

ROMANS 3:23–24, NIV

My Princess...
YOU NEED REST

I know you often grow weary. I hear your heartfelt cry for more energy to make it through each day. You, My tired princess, must trust Me with all your many worries and responsibilities. Rest when I tell you to. I am your heavenly Father, and I know what My girl needs. So listen to the One who loves you the most and knows all about you. I want you to take a step of faith by setting aside a day each week to rest from all your work. If you will obey Me in this, I will multiply your time and supernaturally energize your efforts to get everything done in the following days. Welcome this opportunity to give your mind, body, and spirit a rest. Consider it My love gift to you, and relax in Me!

Love,

Your King and your Resting Place

THEN JESUS SAID, "COME TO ME,
ALL OF YOU WHO ARE WEARY AND CARRY
HEAVY BURDENS, AND I WILL GIVE YOU REST."

MATTHEW 11:28

My Princess...
YOUR TIME IS VALUABLE

The time I have given you is of eternal importance. Your life matters, and the most valuable asset you can give to someone or something is time. Remember, My royal one, I want all of your appointments to be in My perfect will. Not all good opportunities are from Me. Keep in mind, My love, that there may be many ways to make more money, but you can never buy back time. So invest your time wisely. Think about what you are doing and how you spend your precious life. Are your days full of the things that matter most to you? Now is the time to take control of your schedule and live a life that matters. If you will sit with Me, I will help you remove the things that are holding you back from doing what's most needed in this season of your life. There is never a wrong time to do the right thing, so come and experience success with divine direction.

Love,
Your King and Eternal Timekeeper

Our people should learn

to spend their time doing something

useful and worthwhile.

TITUS 3:14, CEV

My Princess...
YOU ARE A VESSEL FOR HONOR

I am the Master Potter, and you are the clay. I know your desire is to be shaped by Me—to be used by Me. That is what I created you for—to be a vessel of honor. I want to fill you up with My love, My hope, My blessing, and pour you out to quench a thirsty world. Even on those days when you feel broken and empty, I can still use you—as long as you are firmly held in My grasp. I chose you because you have seen your own brokenness and have given every shattered piece to Me. No one can become a vessel of honor by sitting tall and pretty—filled to the brim with pride and self-confidence. Don't be afraid to empty yourself of what you think is valuable, and let Me fill you up with what is *invaluable*. Let Me hold you. Let Me fill you. Let Me pour out My blessings *through* you, and you will experience overflowing joy as My vessel of honor.

Love,

Your King and your Creator

If anyone cleanses himself from these things,

he will be a vessel for honor,

sanctified, useful to the Master,

prepared for every good work.

2 TIMOTHY 2:21, NASB

I pray that from his glorious,

unlimited resources he will give you mighty

inner strength through his Holy Spirit.

EPHESIANS 3:16

My Princess...
I CAN KEEP YOU FROM FALLING

I want to do more for you than keep you from evil. I want to free your heart from the desire to sin. When you are being tempted, take authority over evil and speak My words of deliverance out loud—you will discover that My power is greater than the enemy's of your soul. I am your Power, your Safety. I can keep you on the road to everlasting life and let nothing destroy My perfect will for you. I have set you apart for a purpose far greater than any pleasure this world has to offer. So call to Me before you stumble into a trap, and I will make a way of escape. Seek Me, and I will give you the power to prevail. The more you taste of My goodness, the less you will crave any temporary temptation. I am strong in your every weakness, and I will give you strength to walk through or away from any situation. Now get up and go in My name, and let Me help you live a balanced life.

Love,

Your King and your Keeper

My Princess...
I WANT YOU TO BE CONTENT

*Y*ou were given My peace when you let Me into your life. It *is* possible, My princess, to enjoy your life with a peaceful mind and a contented heart. You have so much to look forward to when you're settled in your heavenly home with Me. But for now you must remember that nothing you buy or collect will calm your spirit or soothe your soul like I can. You came into this world with nothing, and that is how you will leave it. Let Me do more than give you the good gifts this life has to offer. I will give you a place of peace, decorated with delight and filled with memories that will be more cherished than anything this world has to offer. So let Me be your treasure, and I will give you a rich life that will become more beautiful than anything money can buy.

Love,

Your King and your Contentment

I know what it is to be in need,
and I know what it is to have plenty.
I have learned the secret of being
content in any and every situation,
whether well fed or hungry,
whether living in plenty or in want.
I can do everything through him
who gives me strength.

PHILIPPIANS 4:12–13, NIV

My Princess...
HAVE A PASSION FOR MY WORD

I want you to have a passion in your heart for Me and My written Word. I promise you…the more you read My word, the more you will want Me. Don't let anyone or anything steal that time away from you and Me, My child. I know you love Me, but I often find you looking everywhere else except to Me. It's My word that lets you live life with supernatural wisdom. It's My word that defines who you are and how much I love you. I know there is much to see and do, but nothing will give you the blessings or security that you will discover in the love letter I've written for you—My Word. Open your Bible today, and let Me reveal Myself to you in a very real and intimate way. Any time you spend with Me will be multiplied by My mighty hand, so draw near to Me and I will draw near to you.

Love,

Your King and your Living Word

Your word is

a lamp to my feet

and a light

for my path.

PSALM 119:105, NIV

My Princess...
LEAD THE LOST

I am dwelling in you and with you. Because My power is in your life, you have the ability to show the way to all who need to find Me. But you won't discover My power or complete your calling if you try and build your life on your own accomplishments. You have been handpicked by Me to refresh a world that is wandering around in a dry and thirsty land. There are many who are lost and feel very alone. Their cups are empty and so are their souls. So let Me fill you with My Spirit, My appointed one; I will show you how to bring them living water and lead them to the true love they long for. I will make a way for you to lead them to Me. And because you loved and followed Me, you will be the one they'll thank on the other side of eternity for showing them the way to heaven.

Love,

Your King who refreshes and leads

And so God can always point to us
as examples of the incredible wealth
of his favor and kindness toward us,
as shown in all he has done for us
through Christ Jesus.

EPHESIANS 2:7

My Princess...
ASK ME ANYTHING

I am all-powerful, and I am preparing you for something significant in My eternal plan. Don't be afraid to dream big just because of past disappointments. Remember, it wasn't your faith in *Me* that failed you, it was your faith in people that caused the pain of broken dreams. I am your King, and I can do anything you ask in My name. King David started out as a small shepherd boy, but had faith big enough to kill a giant. I am just as real today in *you* as I was back then. So ask Me, obey Me, and seek Me with all your heart, mind, and strength. And then watch My promises to you come to pass in my perfect time.

Love,

Your King and Answer to everything

Yes, ask anything in my name,

and I will do it!

JOHN 14:14

My Princess...
CONFESS YOUR SIN TO ME

I love it when you come to Me to confess your sin. I am your safe place and your salvation. My child, there is nothing you can tell Me that I can't handle hearing. I already know your every thought, action, and motive, so why waste even a moment trying to hide any sin from Me? Let's make it right together. Let Me have the thing that's holding you back from the blessed life you desire to live. I am always ready to restore your soul to a place of peace and make you white as snow. Please come to Me in truth and be transparent with your Savior—the Lover of your soul. Let's talk together, and let Me take the weight of your sin. Come to Me in confession and I will wash you clean, and your mind, body, and spirit will know My total healing!

Love,

Your King and Savior who died for you

Finally, I confessed all my sins to you and
stopped trying to hide them.
I said to myself, "I will confess my rebellion
to the LORD." And you forgave me!
All my guilt is gone.

PSALM 32:5

*W*hat this means is that those who become
Christians become new persons.
They are not the same anymore,
for the old life is gone.
A new life has begun!

2 CORINTHIANS 5:17

My Princess...
YOU ARE A NEW CREATION

*Y*ou are My precious daughter, and now that My spirit lives within you, I long to teach you about who you are. Let Me start by defining what you are not, My love. You are *not* a slave to sin any longer. You are no longer under Satan's power. You are not even your own because I bought you with My life.

As your Father, I'm asking you to set a higher standard for yourself. Let go of the old habits that are holding you back from becoming the new you. I can't take you to the next level of your faith until you're willing to receive My instruction. Just as I asked Abraham to leave his comfort zone and go to unfamiliar territory, I am leading you away from your former life. And then I invite you to enter into My presence and receive My power to transform your life.

Love,

Your King who gives new life

My Princess...
I WILL WORK OUT WHAT'S BEST

I know what's best for you, and nothing happens without My knowledge. I see your disappointment when things don't unfold in your life the way you had envisioned. But if you could only lift your eyes to heaven and see My hand moving with eternal purposes, you could better understand. Don't forget that your life here is temporary…in other words, My love, you're not home yet. But for now I want you to trust Me in your disappointments, and let Me turn your pain into a passion to persevere. Wait on Me, My love. Don't give up! Rather, give in to Me and My perfect plan for you, knowing that I only desire the very best for you.

Love,

Your King and Father who truly knows best

The LORD watches over you—
the LORD is your shade at
your right hand.

PSALM 121:5, NIV

My Princess...
I HAVE SET YOU APART

I have called you to be set apart, just as I called those who came before you. I know this calling will sometimes come with great cost, but the eternal rewards are priceless and beyond comparison. Just as I did with Queen Esther, I have given you the ability to walk in such a way so all will see that you are divinely Mine. Some will admire you for your dedication to Me, and some will want you to fail rather than follow your lead. You may fall because you are not perfect, but your mistakes can be the tutors that make you wiser. Don't put pressure on yourself to be perfect. I'm the only one who can perfect you, My princess. All I ask is that you let Me set you apart so that I use you as a witness for the world to see.

Love,

Your King who sets you apart

"I knew you before I formed you
in your mother's womb.
Before you were born
I set you apart and appointed you
as my spokesman to the world."

JEREMIAH 1:5

My Princess...
IT'S OKAY TO CRY

I see how hard you try to handle your heart, and I know you want to live a life without heartaches or pain. I'm asking you to take a step closer to your Father in heaven by crying out to Me when you hurt. Let Me heal you. Remember My chosen, King David? He cried out to Me in his fears, disappointments, and sin, and I answered. You are also My chosen one, and you are My daughter...so it's okay to cry. I don't expect you to pretend that pain is not real. It is truth and tears that will give you the freedom that I want you to know. Now let go of that part of your heart that only I can heal. Let your heavenly Daddy hold you while you cry.

Love,

Your King who wipes away your tears

THOSE WHO SOW IN TEARS WILL REAP WITH SONGS OF JOY.

PSALM 126:5, NIV

My Princess...
GIVE ME CONTROL

I am your King and the ruler of all things. When the winds blow and the waves crash against the sides of your lifeboat, let Me steer you to safety. I'm not only the Captain of your ship, I can also control the storm. I know you like to feel you're in control by holding on to the wheel with all your strength, but I have you and your future under control. Who knows you better than I do? I don't want you to keep exhausting yourself trying to rebuild your life after another shipwreck. I am the One who takes what is broken and rebuilds it even better than before. So give your life back to Me. I will calm you in the storm, or I will clear the rough waters; either way, you will be safe with Me!

Love,

Your King who calms the storm

The disciples woke him up, shouting,

"Master, Master we're going to drown!"

So Jesus rebuked the wind and the raging waves.

The storm stopped and all was calm!

LUKE 8:24

My Princess...
GIVE OF YOURSELF

I see how you pour yourself out to people. I love your heart and how you extend a helping hand to those in need. You will discover the true source of serenity and joy every time you step outside of yourself and give your life for My sake. I want you to remember you can never outgive Me, My love. Anything you do or say to further My Kingdom will be given back to you abundantly. Now go…give your gifts of time and tenderness to a world that desperately needs a touch from Me through you.

Love,

Your King and giver of life

*If anyone gives you
even a cup of water
because you belong to the Messiah,
I assure you, that person
will be rewarded.*

MARK 9:41

My Princess...
COUNT THE COST

I gave My all for you, My love. I gave Myself and died on the cross for you. Your precious soul was worth it all. When I cried out to My Father in heaven to "forgive them, they know not what they have done," I meant you! I know how life challenges you daily, and that sometimes it's hard to see My presence in your stress-filled days. But just think about this, My child: When you see the beautiful heavens I've passionately prepared for you, then you'll say without a doubt that it was worth the cost to live out your life for Me. My Kingdom is the one sure thing worth investing in. Remember, My love, I placed you here by My divine plan, so before you commit to anything or anyone, count the cost—because you are priceless!

Love,

Your King who paid the price for you

The ransom for a life is costly,

no payment is ever enough.

PSALM 49:8, NIV

My Princess...
BE REAL WITH ME

*Y*ou are precious and beautiful to Me. You never need to pretend to be something other than who I made you to be. I don't want you to try to impress Me by pretending that all is perfect in your life, My love. I want you to find great freedom in being real with Me. The more real you become, the better you will relate to others. No more pretending, My princess. I love you just the way you are, and I want you to be real with Me in all you do and say. I gave My life for you so you could live free to be yourself. Don't let anyone steal your joy by turning you into something fake. Be true to yourself and be true to Me, because I love the real you.

Love,

Your True King

NOW THE LORD IS THE SPIRIT,
AND WHERE THE SPIRIT OF THE LORD IS,
THERE IS FREEDOM.

2 CORINTHIANS 3:17 , NIV

DO NOT LET ANY UNWHOLESOME
TALK COME OUT OF YOUR MOUTHS,
BUT ONLY WHAT IS HELPFUL FOR
BUILDING OTHERS UP ACCORDING
TO THEIR NEEDS, THAT IT MAY
BENEFIT THOSE WHO LISTEN.

EPHESIANS 4:29, NIV

My Princess...
GUARD YOUR TONGUE

*R*emember, My love, your tongue has the power of life and death. Every day you will be faced with the opportunity to talk about others. I'm asking you to let Me take control of your conversations. When you are tempted to give in to gossip, pray. I'm the only One who can tame your tongue. I know how hard it is to think before you speak, but I will help you. I want you to be careful who you listen to and what conversations you engage in. Socializing with the wrong people and getting involved with useless conversation or harmful hearsay can cost you friendships and your reputation. I am willing to listen to all that concerns you about others. So talk to Me first, and I will give you words of wisdom in how to build up others and glorify Me.

Love,

Your King who purifies your tongue

"*Forget the former things;*

do not dwell on the past.

See, I am doing a new thing!"

ISAIAH 43:18–19, NIV

My Princess...
LET GO OF GUILT

All have sinned and fallen short of My glory, so why won't you forgive yourself when you fall? Don't you know that I will pick you up when you call out to Me and repent? There is no wrong that can keep Me, your King, from redeeming you back to your royal life again. Read My Word, My love; many of My chosen ones made mistakes. Just as I gave each of them a new start, so will I do the same for you. This is a new day, and I am ready to do a new thing in you. Now, let go of guilt, and trust Me to work out what went wrong. Just watch Me make you into the person I called you to be. I am the God of second chances, and My mercy endures forever!

Love,

Your King who removes your guilt

My Princess...
SET YOUR BOUNDARIES

Come to Me, My precious, when you feel out of control and overextended. I want to take you to a place where you can be still and reflect on your life. I did not call you to be everything to everyone. You have placed that demand on yourself. Even My son, Jesus, needed to walk away from the demands of the crowd and find comfort alone with Me. Let's write out what really matters most to you, so we can draw some boundaries to preserve your peace of mind and purpose for living. Even I drew the boundaries around the mighty ocean. It's good to take control of your valuable time and realize it's all right to say no. That one word will deliver you from a life of pressure to a place of amazing control and peace.

Love,

Your King who knows your boundaries

*M*ark out a straight path for your feet;
then stick to the path and stay safe.
Don't get sidetracked;
keep your feet from following evil.

PROVERBS 4:26-27

My Princess...
GO WHERE I SEND YOU

*Y*ou seek Me for your place in this world, and My answer to you is wherever you are standing. I love to hear you pray to be used by Me. Nothing pleases Me more than when your love flows warm and free. When you're willing, I am ready to strategically place you somewhere to be a blessing. Even the smallest effort can lift the burden of someone else when you are living by My power. You won't always understand why I send you to do things that no one else will see, but you don't work for others—you work for Me. What you do now will be seen by all on the other side of eternity. So go where I send you today, knowing that I have prepared the way.

Love,

Your King who is the Way

BE STRONG AND STEADY, ALWAYS ENTHUSIASTIC ABOUT THE LORD'S WORK, FOR YOU KNOW THAT NOTHING YOU DO FOR THE LORD IS EVER USELESS.

1 CORINTHIANS 15:58

My Princess...
TAKE CARE OF YOUR TEMPLE

*M*y love, you are My special treasure. You are My royal temple, and I—your King—dwell within you. I created you to be a royal, holy place where My Holy Spirit lives. I want you to be a glorious, shining example of My handiwork for the entire world to see. Although your eternal King resides in you, your body is still in need of rest. Take time for yourself; your mental and spiritual health depend on it. You're not being selfish by doing this, so don't let others make you feel guilty about your decision. My princess, you and I will work in complete harmony with a divine purpose and a royal commission—to touch the hearts of those around you. In your quiet times, My precious one, come into My presence, and let Me refresh your temple with My spiritual strength. It is My good pleasure to give you all you need.

Love,

Your King and your Caretaker

*Don't you know that
you yourselves are God's temple
and that God's Spirit lives in you?
If anyone destroys God's temple,
God will destroy him;
for God's temple is sacred,
and you are that temple.*

1 CORINTHIANS 3:16–17, NIV

My Princess...
LOVE IS NOT A GAME

Listen to Me, My princess. Love is not a game—it is a gift. I know there are those who don't sincerely care for your heart, but I say that your heart is priceless. Reflect on your relationships, My royal one. Who are you allowing into your private world? Do they draw you closer to Me, or do they weaken your faith in Me and draw you away? I gave My life so you could be free. I don't want you to play "relational games" to get the approval of people. If you choose to play these games, you will miss out on all I have for you. I am your Father, and I know what's right for My daughter. Hold on to Me and let go of those who harm you. Then you'll be free from their power, and you'll be wise enough to see what a real, lasting relationship is meant to be.

Love,

Your King who bought you

You are not your own;
you were bought at a price.
Therefore honor God
with your body.

1 CORINTHIANS 6:19–20, NIV

My Princess...
ACCEPT OTHERS

*Y*ou, My unique princess, are your own special person. The way you think and the talents you have are a gift from Me. I did not give you this gift to compare yourself to others or to condemn others. No one is *you!* I want you to look around and see the way I colored the world with different kinds of people. The glory of My creation is seen in the details and in the differences. The beauty of relationships is found when different gifts and temperaments come together in My harmony. Your purpose is not to mold others to be like you, but to help them to open their own gifts by accepting them the way I accept you. Remember, My pretty princess, I gave you a talent to touch others—not to tear them down.

Love,

Your King and your Ultimate Gift

There are different kinds of gifts,
but the same Spirit.

1 CORINTHIANS 12:4, NIV

My Princess...
YOU ARE MY MASTERPIECE

I love what I have created. I am delighted in you!

Don't ever feel insecure about what you think you are not, because I made you in My image and your uniqueness is a gift from Me. I did not give you a life, My love, for you to squeeze into a man-made mold. You are royalty, but you won't discover that truth by gazing into a mirror. Let Me be your mirror and I will reflect back to you your true beauty. The more you gaze at Me, the more you will see My workmanship in you. The sooner you see yourself for who you really are, the sooner you can begin your reign as My priceless princess with a purpose.

Love,

Your King and your Creator

For we are God's masterpiece,
He created us anew in Christ Jesus so that
we can do the good things he planned
for us long ago.

EPHESIANS 2:10

MAY YOU EXPERIENCE THE LOVE
OF CHRIST, THOUGH IT IS SO GREAT
YOU WILL NEVER FULLY UNDERSTAND IT.
THEN YOU WILL BE FILLED
WITH THE FULLNESS OF LIFE
AND POWER THAT COMES
FROM GOD.

EPHESIANS 3:19

My Princess...
I LOVE YOU
BEYOND DESCRIPTION

*T*here are no words to describe how much I love you. That is why I stretched out My arms of love and died for you. I know sometimes you don't feel lovable, but you don't have to earn My affection. I adore you. You are My creation. I never want you to doubt My commitment to you.

I am the Lover of your soul, so let Me meet your every need. I long to set you free from searching for false love in the wrong places. Let Me hold on to your heart and fill you up with eternal love. Then you will feel My Holy presence and fall in love with Me.

Love,

Your King who can't stop loving you

My Princess...
YOU HAVE A
HOME IN HEAVEN

$\mathcal{D}$id you know that I have prepared a home for you in heaven? It is more beautiful than you can ever imagine. Your eyes have not seen nor have your ears heard the majestic beauty that awaits you. But for now, My chosen one, I need you to learn to see your life with an eternal perspective. When you cross over into heaven, you won't be able to bring anything from your home here on earth. You're only here to bring forth My life-changing news of salvation. Don't collect things; collect people. I have called you to bring others to Me. Remember, no one will grow closer to Me because of what you *have*. Tell them how much I love them. They need to know about My amazing plans for their lives and about the eternal kingdom that awaits them, too.

Love,
Your King and your Eternity Builder

"NO EYE HAS SEEN, NO EAR HAS HEARD,
AND NO MIND HAS IMAGINED
WHAT GOD HAS PREPARED
FOR THOSE WHO LOVE HIM."

1 CORINTHIANS 2:9

My Princess...
YOU ARE MY DELIGHT

*I*t brings Me great pleasure to see internal beauty blossom inside of you and to watch you grow up in Me. I delight in every moment we spend together. I delight in giving you the desires of your heart. I delight in hearing you call out to Me. Don't ever feel like you're unimportant to Me. There is no reason for you to feel unsure of My love for you. I am always waiting for you to delight yourself in Me and in My love. It is My pleasure to bless you abundantly. Don't look to anyone else to meet your deepest wants and needs, because you will only end up empty and disappointed. Only I can turn your tears into joy and fill the emptiness in your heart. So delight yourself in Me, and you will live life to the fullest because you are My delight.

Love,

Your King and your Lord of Eternal Delight

The steps of the godly
are directed by the LORD.
He delights in every detail
of their lives.

PSALM 37:23

My Princess...
SEEK AFTER ME

I will wait for you as long as it takes. There is nothing that pleases Me more than when you, My princess, seek after Me. Like a lonely traveler seeking shelter from a storm, come to Me. Take comfort under My roof. Find security within My walls. Let Me be your hiding place. That is what I created you for. You were never meant to wander the cold, lonely streets of life alone. So seek Me in the morning, and seek Me throughout the day and into the evening. Pursue Me with all your heart. When you do, you will find more than shelter. You will find a place to lay down your burdens and rest. You will also discover that I have been pursuing you all along.

Love,

Your King and your Shelter

The one thing
I ask of the LORD—
the thing I seek most—
is to live in the house of the LORD
all the days of my life.

PSALM 27:4

*S*ince you excel in so many ways—
you have so much faith, such gifted speakers,
such knowledge, such enthusiasm,
and such love for us—now I want you to excel
also in this gracious ministry of giving.

2 CORINTHIANS 8:7

My Princess...
STRIVE FOR EXCELLENCE

I chose you to set a standard of excellence. Look around you, My loved one. Many have no example of what excellence looks like. You were created to live a life that displays a higher standard. My Spirit in you, combined with your desire to be the best and do the best, has the amazing ability to inspire others to break free from mediocrity. Together, we will encourage them to step into an abundant life of blessings and generous giving. Come to Me every day, and let Me lift you to a level of excellence that is only possible in the supernatural realm. I don't want you to wear yourself out by trying to empower yourself. Remember I am ready and able to equip you with the power and passion to achieve an excellent life.

Love,

Your Generous King

Above all else,
guard your heart,
for it is the wellspring of life.

PROVERBS 4:23, NIV

My Princess...
GUARD YOUR HEART

*I*f I were to hand you a fragile, newborn baby girl, I know that you would protect her with your life. Your arms would be strong, your feet sure, and your eyes ever watchful. Be careful, My trusted one! For I have placed something just as precious and delicate within you. It is your heart...your very life! Treasure it. Protect it. Watch over it with all your strength. For the world and all its pleasures are like kidnappers who will stop at nothing to steal your heart away from Me and destroy it. I want what is best for you, My treasured one, and although you sometimes feel that the sinful pleasures of this world don't seem harmful, they will separate you from Me. Just as a newborn is helpless without loving care, you also will suffer if your heart is taken from Me. So I'm asking you to guard your heart and cling to Me, the Source of your life.

Love,

Your King and your Life Giver

My Princess...
YOU WILL FOREVER BE REMEMBERED

Your life is a treasure that will bless your children's children! I have chosen you, My princess, to carve out the future for the generations that follow your example. Remember, it's your choices, your character, your love and obedience to Me that will live on long after you are gone from this world. My Spirit will continue to give guidance and hope to all who have watched you live out your call. I have covered everything with My blood and have cleansed you from all sin. I want you to discover the joy and purpose of knowing that not only have I called you, I also will live out this great honor with you and through you. When you walk with Me, the model of your life will be more than a memory; it will leave an indelible mark on the hearts and lives of all who loved you. Even their children's children will be blessed because you loved Me.

Love,

Your King and your Future

Happy are those who delight

in doing what he commands.

Their children will be successful everywhere;

an entire generation of godly people will be blessed.

They themselves will be wealthy,

and their good deeds will never be forgotten.

PSALM 112:1–3

"I AM THE ALPHA AND THE OMEGA,
THE BEGINNING AND THE END.
TO HIM WHO IS THIRSTY
I WILL GIVE TO DRINK
WITHOUT COST FROM THE SPRING
OF THE WATER OF LIFE."

REVELATION 21:6, NIV

My Princess...
YOU BEGIN AND END WITH ME

*Y*ou need not worry when your life will end, My precious child. All you need to know is that your first breath began with Me, and your last breath will lead you to My presence. Don't ever let fear of death or eternity frighten you. Your todays and tomorrows are secure with Me—I have held them in My hand since the beginning of time. When you finish your brief time on earth and I call you into My presence, your *forever life* in heaven will begin. But for now, My chosen one, you must live free from fear. Instead, trust Me to take you through every trial that comes your way. Remember that nothing in the universe can separate us. I am with you always…even until the end of time. So live well and finish strong—fixing your hope on the day that we will meet face-to-face on the other side of eternity.

Love,

Your Eternal King

Closing thoughts
FROM THE AUTHOR...

I pray as you have read through these love letters that you have discovered that God's love, power, and promises are for you. But I could not let you close this book without making sure you know the King personally. Because reading about God's love is not enough to secure a place in His eternal kingdom. We need to accept His invitation and receive the gift of His Son Jesus Christ. I would love the privilege of being a part of your eternal crowning by asking you to say this simple prayer with me:

Dear God, I don't want to live without You any longer.
I believe You sent Your Son to die for me and I want Him
to be my Lord and my King. I confess my sin and my need
for a Savior and I accept Your free gift of everlasting life.
I thank You for writing my name in Your book of life.
I pray this prayer by faith in Jesus' name. Amen

If this is your sincere prayer, you can know that angels are rejoicing and the Holy Spirit of the Living God is now in you. If I don't have the honor of meeting you during your reign through this life, I look forward to celebrating with you on the other side of eternity.

Until then, may our King bless your walk with Him.

Love, your sister in Christ,

Sheri Rose

I TELL YOU THE TRUTH,
WHOEVER HEARS MY WORD
AND BELIEVES HIM WHO SENT ME
HAS ETERNAL LIFE AND
WILL NOT BE CONDEMNED;
HE HAS CROSSED OVER
FROM DEATH TO LIFE.

JOHN 5:24

I'd love to HEAR FROM YOU!

To write Sheri Rose personally,
or to book Sheri Rose to speak at your
church or event, or to learn more
about His Princess™ conferences,
visit her website at
www.HisPrincess.com
or call 602-407-8789.

The King Is Awaiting
Your Presence!

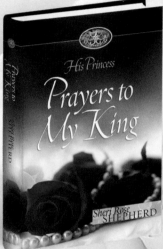

Prayers to My King is a beautiful gift book created
to help women connect intimately with their God.
While the first book in the His Princess™ series reminded
us that we are loved intimately and unconditionally by
our King, this second book helps us express our deepest
thoughts, desires, fears and failures, by crying out to
God through prayer.

978-1-59052-470-1

The Crowning Moment

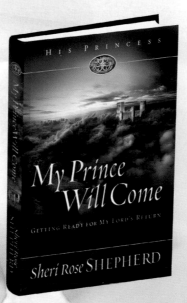

My Prince Will Come is the third book in the His
Princess™ series. Encouraging as it is practical, *My Prince
Will Come* equips every woman to start living today a
life of incredible freedom from the past, joy in the
present, and hope for the future.

978-1-59052-531-9

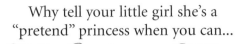

Find out more ways to tell your little girl she is God's princess!

- His Little Princess Conferences
- His Little Princess Tea Sets
- His Little Princess Birthday Party Packs
- His Little Princess Crowns and Jewelry
- His Little Princess News

Visit **www.HisPrincess.com**
or call 602-407-8789 for a free catalog.

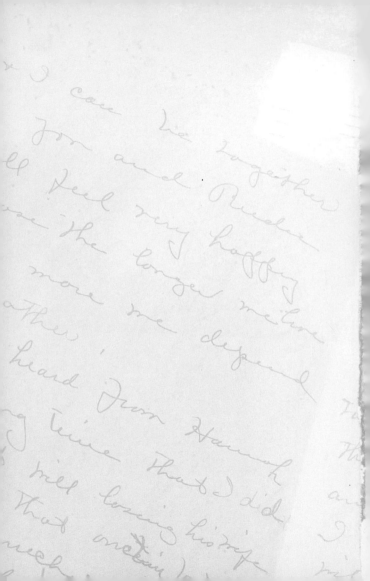